BLOOMERS!

MORE NEWSPAPER MISPRINTS

ILLUSTRATED BY
ROY CARR

BLANDFORD PRESS
POOLE · DORSET

SMILE A WHILE

...an 82 year-old retired mine started married life again yesterday with a bridge of 92.

SUNDAY EXPRESS

PHILLIPS Ultra violent health lamp...

WATFORD EVENING ECHO

The piper and burglar were kindly supplied by the local church.

GLASGOW JEWISH ECHO.

Lost: grey and white car, could be pregnant...

ENFIELD INDEPENDENT

FASHION REPORT

For sale: suede boots, size four, as new, less speakers....

KENT MESSENGER

For sale: Gents skirts, 16 " collar

GLASGOW EVENING TIMES

FINEST PLAID KILTS MADE TO SUIT YOUR OWN REQUIREMENTS

PAY HERE

For sale: girl's turquoise polyester and chiffon dress, 2" chest.

RHYL JOURNAL

Richard Goolden, now in his 84th year, is appearing in Tom Stoppard,s Dirty Linen,
now in its third.

DAILY MAIL

Licencees in the village of Oughterbridge are to be invited to talks with the local gala committee in a bed to reduce the problem of drunks....

THE STAR

GROUP FOR A GIGGLE

The plan is to build a 265-seater elevated grandstand in front of the rifle range.

LANCASHIRE EVENING POST

The Supreme Court has declared that anyone deprived illegally of his life can come before it and ask for compensation.

THE OVERSEAS HINDUSTAN NEWS

He shook his fish in the conductors face

CLAPHAM OBSERVER

It was a most beautiful catch by Hutchings... The tree which stands in the ground
was too near to be pleasant, and Mr Hutchings had to run back quickly and held it over his head.

THE TIMES

'ORSES DOOVERS

The customer seeking the best of international cuisine will be disappointed. *THE PENWITH PIRATE*

Also on the menu is lunch or supper of smoked salmon and boys.

TARGET

Come and try our Greek special ties at our famous restaurant.....

TOURIST GUIDE

Good value restaurants in Hong Kong are Jimmy's Kitchen for lunch and sinner, and Maxim's for lunch only.

BRITISH AIRWAYS BROCHURE

LIVING IN STYLE

Self-contained basement flat, central London, plus small salary return part-time help elderly but youthful quacker lady.

THE LADY

A detached 213 bedroomed bungalow on large corner plot.

SOUTH WALES ECHO

Terraced house, ballroom, lounge, dining room...

BURTON TRADER

Peaceful, relaxing, self-contained, stone built cottages and bungalows....

sandy beach only 300 years away.

WALES HOLIDAYS 1983 BROCHURE

THE RAG TRADE....

They make chick dresses bound for the High street department stores.

DAILY MAIL

I recently bought a pair of arousers in a boutique...

EVENING PRESS (DUBLIN)

A number of briefs were stolen from a washing line. Also missing from the line are a jumper and a kettle.

MACCLESFIELD ADVERTISER

He was supplied with a tweed cap, umbrella and weatherproof jacket to fend off the driving rain at the British Fairy Farming event.

BIRMINGHAM EVENING MAIL

WEATHER PERMITTING

**Weather: Tomorrow, mainly dry.
Milk, with sunny intervals.**

SHROPSHIRE STAR

**A seven hour battle in a Force 7 gale
to get her to safety succeeded only
when a god tracked their scent.**

DAILY EXPRESS

**SNOW REPORT: Cairngorm – No
report because of bad weather.**

GLASGOW HERALD

CAIRNGORM
WEATHER CENTRE

The next 24 hours will continue cold and windy with occasional snow showers, some heavy falls on high ground with drifting in palaces.

NEWCASTLE EVENING CHRONICLE

KIDS KORNER..

The child is available in red, blue, green or gold, from all good high street babyshops.

THE MAIDSTONE EXTRA

Three day trip to Denmark....Kids we throw in free.

NEWS OF THE WORLD

His hay fever caught fire spreading flames which damaged the bed....

BRISTOL EVENING POST

"999 men deliver baby".

KENTISH EXPRESS

WANTED COLUMN...

Ex-head herdsman requires milking...

SUSSEX EXPRESS

SNOOKER table, 88ft x 4ft, slate bed....

EXETER EXPRESS AND ECHO

Wanted: Office furniture and stationary salespeople.

EVENING ARGUS

Lifejackets wanted urgently.....

EVENING CHRONICLE

GRIEVOUS BODILY HARM...

The victim suffered bites to his cheek, thing and ankle.

EVENING HERALD

Imagine my shame when I hit one off the toe and almost decapitated a spectator.

DAILY EXPRESS

...who assaulted a bank messenger with an iron bra.

GUARDIAN

The preacher for next Sunday will be hung in the porch.

WEST CHIPPENHAM SUN

PLAY IT AGAIN SAM..

For sale: Lovely Rosewood piano. Owner going abroad with beautiful twisted legs.

NORTH WALES ADVERTISER

Professional person, late twenties to thirties, wanted to share house with piano.

LANCASHIRE EVENING POST

Wanted: Uptight piano...

ABERGAVENNY CHRONICLE

The young conductors tackle Beethoven's Erotica Symphony.

SPECIAL OFFERS

**Firewood blocks for sale
also chimmney sweep.**

ROSS SHIRE JOURNAL

**Car trailer, minus axle and
car trailer, minus wheels. Offers.**

CARDIFF POST

Hotpoint Supermatic twin-tub, good education...

EDINBURGH EVENING NEWS

Harris Tweed sports car, fit man 5ft 8in.

BRADFORD STAR

ONE OVER THE EIGHT

She said passengers had received every
attention including free wind and vodka....

WESTERN EVENING HERALD

For sale at the keenest price possible,
500 parcels containing one bottle world
famous Grench Cognac, one bottle of an
excellent Scotch Wishky, one bottle of
perfume and a surprice...

ALGEMEEN DAGBLAD (ROTTERDAM)

This way you can drink a good deal,
keep cool, and not get inebriated
under the hot sin.

SIGNATURE

A Burnley man drank all day after a win on the horses and ended up by smashing three widows while walking home.

EVENING STAR

FOOD FOR THOUGHT...

People who eat eight ounces of fist every day of the year....

SUNDAY INDEPENDENT

Ecko Hostess with four food compartments and plate wormer....

EASTBOURNE GAZETTE

Twenty residents had an unexpected Sunday breakfast.... teat and toast in a Liverpool police station.

LIVERPOOL ECHO

Fish and Ships, Town centre.

BOURNEMOUTH INFORMER

SNIP BUYS...

For sale: a cross-cut saw by a Willard man with newly sharpened teeth.

WILLARD COMPANY NEWS

Two very nice maternity socks, good quality...

THE CHASE POST

Complete home for sale..three piece suite wireless, television, carpets, lion etc...

PORTSMOUTH EVENING NEWS

18cwt solitaire engagement ring, £80 ono...

BRISTOL EVENING POST

IT'S A STEAL...

Valuables were taken from a downstairs room while the occupiers were asleep in two cases.

EASTERN DAILY EXPRESS

Bag snatched by a man in his 20's. It contained a 71 year-old woman....

MANCHESTER EVENING NEWS

On Sunday morning, cooks smashed the glass in the front door of a video shop....

ENFIELD ADVERTISER

...her dog chased a prowler out of her yard last night.
She said he fired two shots at the fleeing suspect.

SCOTTSDALE PROGRESS

COME FLY WITH ME

Eight young people have just finished six months raining with British Aerospace...

WELWYN & HATFIELD EXPRESS

RAF men wee standing around the plane...

DAILY MAIL

The air forces....are within weeks on their requirements for a new all-weather lighter.

SUNDAY EXPRESS

The organisers...trust you will watch the airfield pass over your area.

CHICHESTER OBSERVER

FINAL RESULT

United trooped off with their pride in taters...

SUNDAY PEOPLE

**Muchiki was pinned on the ropes taking
mire punches to both head and body...**

DAILY MIRROR

**He and his opponent made 30
breads in the next game.**

BRISTOL EVENING POST

No sooner had the race been completed than she was out winning another gold meal for Britain.

DAILY MAIL

Here is the News..

Ireland has become a major international
base for large scale peddling of hard rugs.

IRISH PRESS

Six girls struggled from sick-beds
on Tuesday for a last minute rehearsal
for the final ceremony and downed their
swimsuits.

SINGAPORE TIMES

The committee heard that various bodies
had highlighted the problem of road safety.

BRAINTREE AND WITHAM TIMES

They were taken to hospital after their inflatable boat overturned. At one stage it was thought that one of them might have lost an ear as they struggled to retreive it as it went round in circles.

SCARBOROUGH MERCURY

STRANGE SIGHTS

There may well be some good news for people who were using hand-held horses to water their gardens.

THE SUN (SYDNEY)

A retired army colonel said he saw her on July 20, looking distinguished with a goatee and mustache.

NEWHAVEN REGISTER (CONNECTICUT)

He was, for a number of ears, manager of the Leeds branch.

YORKSHIRE POST

He works high in the Border hills repairing power cables which means he exercises his legs by shining up poles every day.

DAILY STAR

SITUATIONS VACANT

Electrician wanted for shoplifting work..

YORKSHIRE EVENING POST

...Clerk..required by small but busty accounts office.

SHROPSHIRE STAR

..the sucessful candidate must be flexible and able to work under pleasure.

SOUTHERN EVENING ECHO

Mothers Help wanted to help with children and lighthouse work.

EAST GRINSTEAD NEWS IN FOCUS

HOTEL TALES...

The licensee of the Ring O' Bells
Bradford has come second in the
Joshua Tetley Pup of the Year Contest.

BRADFORD TELEGRAPH & ARGUS

Royal Hotel,
only 58, four nights
bed and fast.

SUNDAY POST

J & TR welcome you to their lice, family hotel.

ABERDARE LEADER

The Dolphin & Anchor Hotel require a mad couple to manage a busy high-class bar.

CATERER AND HOTEL KEEPER

LOCAL ENTERTAINMENT

...inside the Guildhall was
a Martian Arts Exhibition.

WESTERN EVENING HERALD

...he is deep in discussions
for a film of his navel.

THE SCOTSMAN

In printing yesterday the name of one of the musical
comedies which the Bandmaster Company is presenting
next week as The Grill in the Train, what our compositor
meant to set was, the Girl in the Drain.

SOUTH CHINA MORNING POST

..the visiting lecturer next week will be Professor Hugh Trevor Roper, well known for his research on Adolf Hitler who will talk about Sir Walter Scott.

YORKSHIRE POST

SAY THAT AGAIN...

Suddenly a fish flashed and Day collapsed. The referee saw nothing but the linesman did.

SUNDAY EXPRESS

...you may feel that it would be right for you to be paid into a bank.

NATIONAL GIROBANK BROCHURE

The North...people...eat most eggs and fish but consume the least cheese and mink.

DAILY MAIL

Audrey...is a registered danger with the Scottish Official Board of Highland Dancing,...

FALKIRK HERALD

IT'S A FAIR COP...

The Grime Prevention Squad based at Burton police station.....

BURTON DAILY MAIL

Christchurch police took a herd of young bull heifers into custody early today after the animals got the wanderlust.

BOURNEMOUTH EVENING ECHO

Police have booked nearly 700 drivers in two months for diving more than 80mph on the

DAILY TELEGRAPH

He also admitted an assault which caused bodily harm to the Police sergeant who sustained a large wheel across his back.

LEIGH REPORTER AND GOLBORNE STAR

Recipe for Laughter...

MENU - Ducking a l'Orange.

CUMBERNAULD NEWS

"First catch your hair," runs the old recipe for jugged hair.

DAILY EXPRESS

....complete frozen meals, the kind that just need warming through in the oven, for about two years.

SCARBOROUGH TOP TRADER

Chocolate potato cake: 6oz margarine, 1oz cocoa, 4oz warm mashed potato, 5oz self-raising flour, 433 eggs, size 3....

WOMANS WEEKLY

SPOT THE BALL...

Two foals in four minutes....gave them avictory they did not deserve.

SUNDAY EXPRESS

Prayers for Garston-based Sunday league football team urgently wanted

LIVERPOOL MERSEYMART

He placed the ball in the net and his delighted team mates couldn't believe their lunch had finally changed.

LIVERPOOL ECHO

The King of Egypt's chief butler was not a bad man but for some reason he had displeased this despotic monarch who promtly put him in goal.

CHRISTIAN HERALD

PLEASE FOLLOW THE INSTRUCTIONS

Before baking, be sure to line your pants with aluminium foil and butter them.
BELDON TIMES

Send your story along with a stamped addressed envelope and a recent photograph or yourself.
MY WEEKLY

The authorities at Ongar library have received a number of complaints about a card in the index file with an entry which read: SEX: SEE LIBRARIAN This has now been changed. The new entry reads: SEX: FOR SEX ASK AT THE DESK.
EASTERN GAZETTE

The best you can do is to slow down and ride for a bit out of the saddle.
(The same technique can be used for breaking wind)

BICYCLE

SPRING SALE

For sale: Single divan wrist watch, with headboard.

NELSON LEADER

For sale: Mothercare baby, as new....

DISS EXPRESS

For sale: Bedroom unit consisting of full-size bed on top of small wardrobe and desk.

SLOUGH OBSERVER

For sale: automatic projector and scream in good condition.

ILKESTON AND HEANOR SHOPPER

GIS' A JOB...

Yes, there is a possibility of a duel career in wood and photography.

DAILY EXPRESS

I am currently in a job with responsibility but I feel I need a change.
I am 22 and a quick leaner.

BOLTON EVENING NEWS

Senior ex-pat with 10 years Middle East experience seeks position in air conditioning or refrigeration.

GULF DAILY NEWS

All the men want is a national ballet.

DAILY MAIL

First published in the U.K. 1984 by Blandford Press, Link House, West Street, Poole, Dorset BH15 1LL

Copyright © 1984 Roy Carr

ISBN 0 7137 1560 X

Printed and bound in Great Britain by Purnell & Sons Ltd., Paulton, Somerset.